Peru Fun Facts Picture Book for Kids

An Educational City Travel Photography Photobook About History, Places with Everything You Need to Know About the Country for Children & Teens

No part of this book may be copied, reproduced or sold without express permission from the owner.
copyright ALPHA ZURIEL PUBLISHING © 2022. All rights reserved

Geography

Peru, the third-largest country in South America, is located on the central western coast of the continent facing the Pacific Ocean. The country shares a land border with Brazil, Bolivia, Chile, Colombia, and Ecuador. It shares the longest land border with Brazil. It has many landscapes ranging from mountains to beaches, deserts, and rainforests. Lima is the capital city of Peru.

History

It was about 15,000 years ago that the first set of people arrived in the country, making the country very old. There have been different societies on the west coast for over 5000 years ago. These societies included the Chavín, the Nasca, and the Moche and began spreading Inland.

The Inca people were one of the most important in the Peruvian culture. They lived there for about six centuries, built Machu Picchu, a famous city in the Andes, and their capital, Cusco, is still in existence. Peru proclaimed its independence from Spain on 28 July 1821.

PERU FUN FACTS

The Mighty Amazon River begins In Peru.

Climate

Peru's climate is different because of its diverse geographical conditions. The coastal desert strips have a mild climate, cloudy winters, and cool, warm summers. The Andean Zone is cold depending on the altitude, and the large areas of the Amazonian forest in the east have a hot, humid climate all year round.

People

The inhabitants of Peru are a mix of Spaniards, Indians, Asians, and Europeans. Peru's largest ethnic group is mestizo. Other groups include Quechuas, Europeans, Aymaras, and Amazonians.

About 80% of Peruvians speak Peruvian Spanish. Quechua, Aymara, and English are other popular languages. The literacy rate in the country is about 94%. Catholicism is the major religion in Peru.

Peruvians dislike making others feel awkward. They are calm and avoid conflict wherever possible. You'll notice they are concerned about their appearances and would not say anything that might reflect poorly on them.

Culture

Amerindian, European, and African civilizations are all blended within Peruvian culture. Because of the country's ethnic variety, many traditions and customs may coexist harmoniously. A vital part of Peruvian culture is music and dancing. The culture is expressed in various ways, including food, music, art, and architecture.

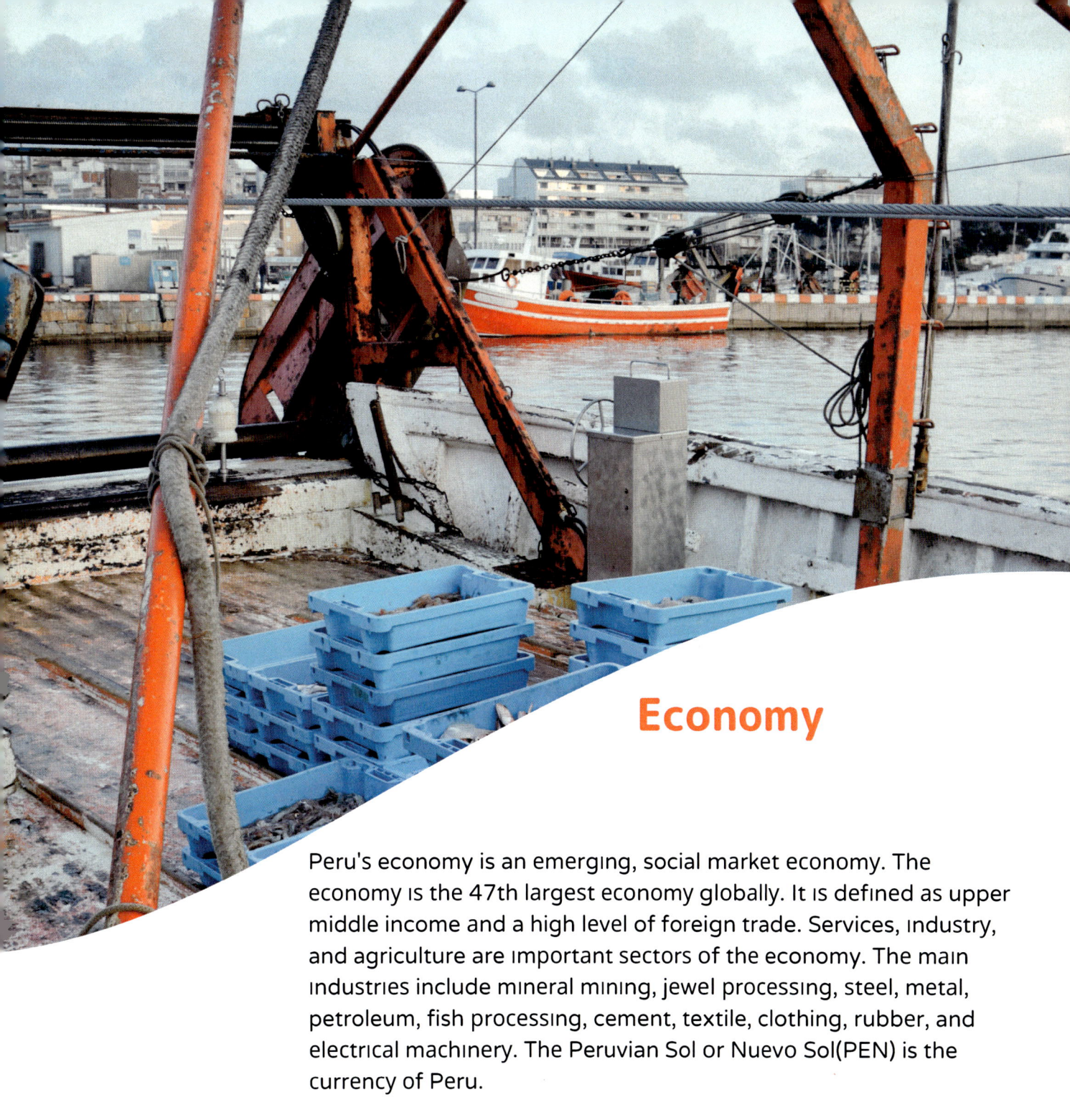

Economy

Peru's economy is an emerging, social market economy. The economy is the 47th largest economy globally. It is defined as upper middle income and a high level of foreign trade. Services, industry, and agriculture are important sectors of the economy. The main industries include mineral mining, jewel processing, steel, metal, petroleum, fish processing, cement, textile, clothing, rubber, and electrical machinery. The Peruvian Sol or Nuevo Sol(PEN) is the currency of Peru.

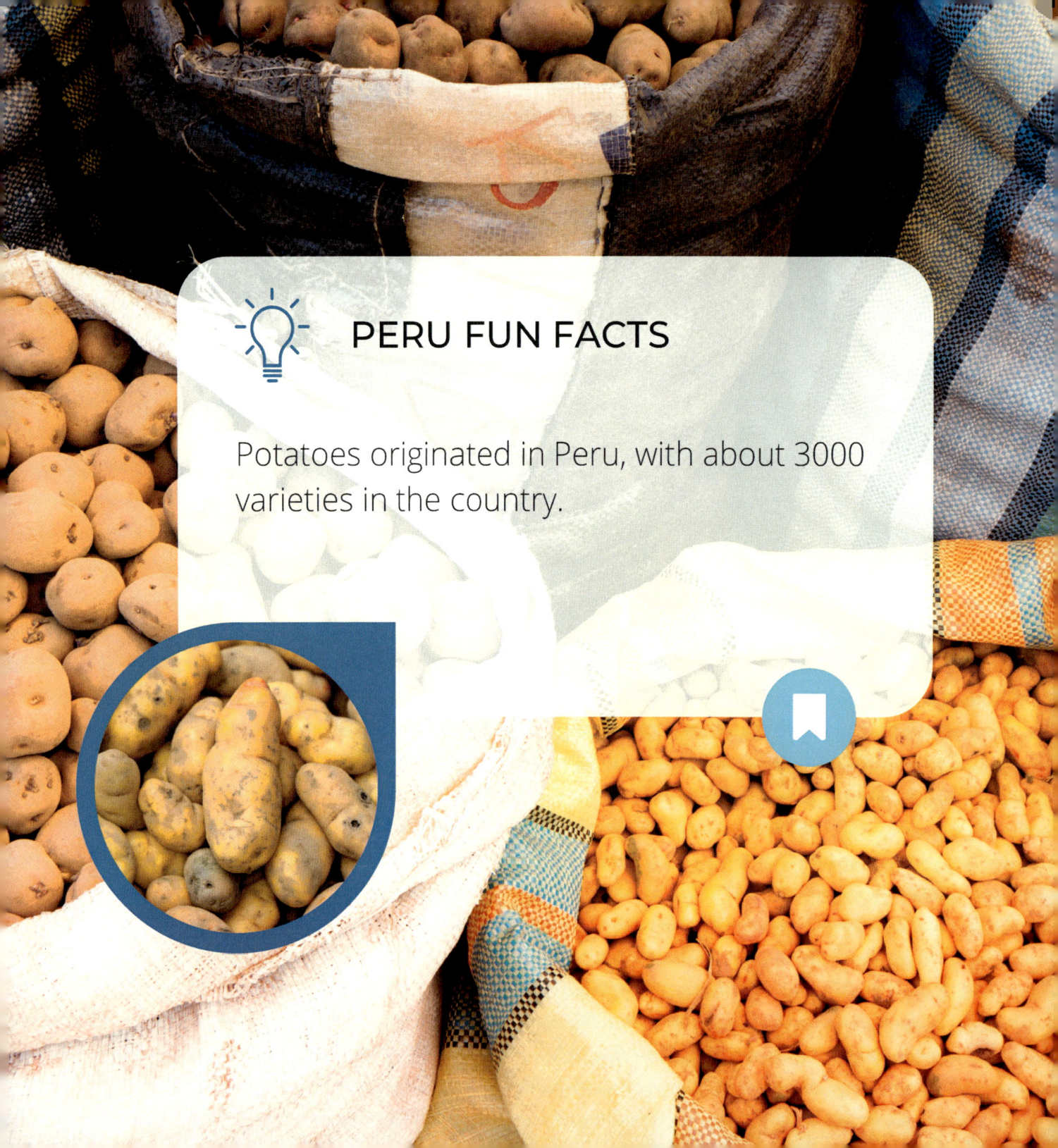

PERU FUN FACTS

Potatoes originated in Peru, with about 3000 varieties in the country.

Public Holidays

New Year's Day- Jan 1st
Easter Holidays
Labor Day- May 1st
Inti Raymi- Jun 24
Saint Peter and Saint Paul-Jun 29
Independence Day: Jul 28-29
Santa Rosa de Lima- Aug 30
Battle of Angamos-Oct 8
All Saints' Day-Nov 1
Immaculate Conception Day-Dec 8
Battle of Ayacucho-Dec 9
Christmas Holidays

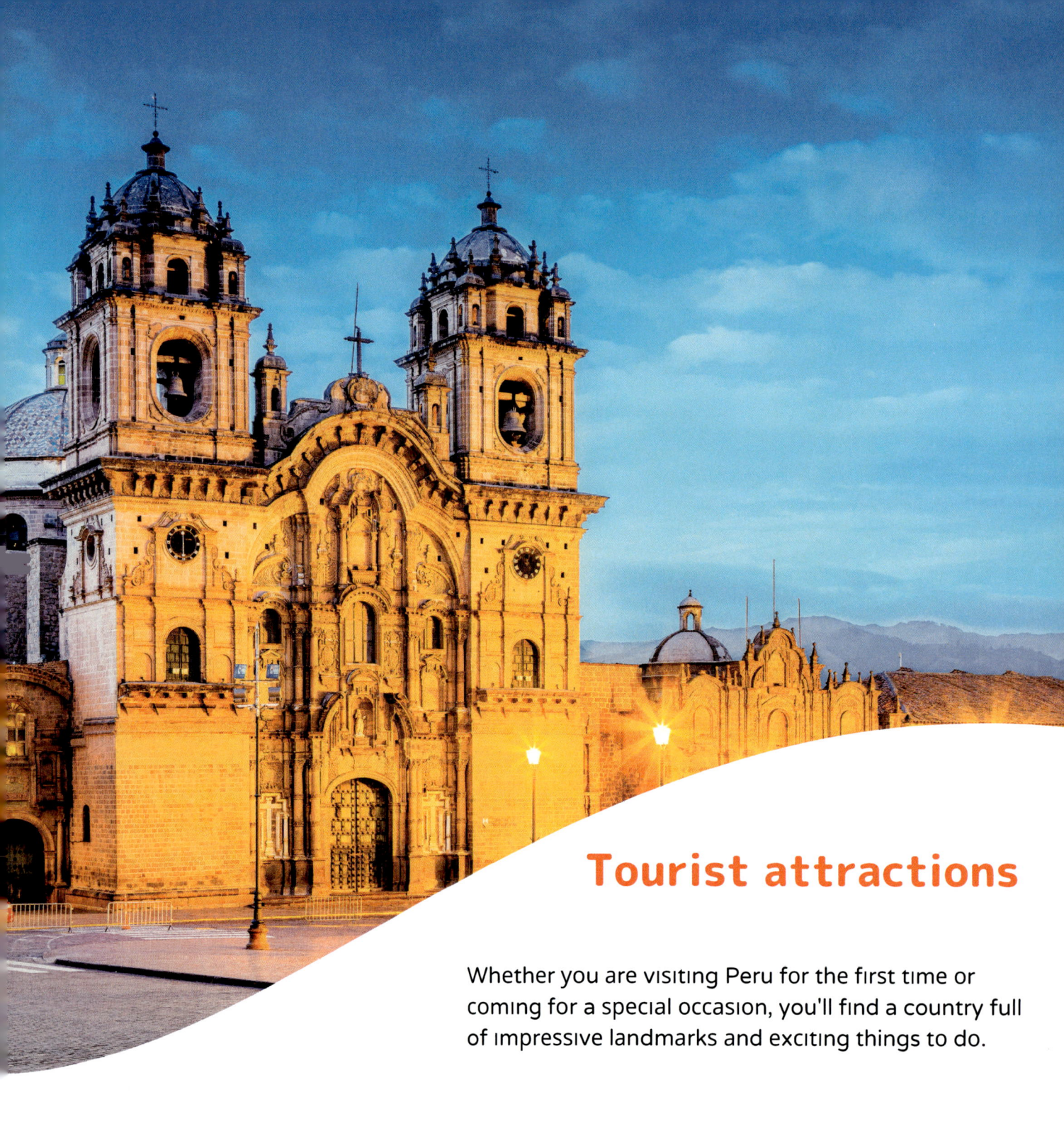

Tourist attractions

Whether you are visiting Peru for the first time or coming for a special occasion, you'll find a country full of impressive landmarks and exciting things to do.

Machu Picchu

Machu Picchu is a beautiful ancient site globally. Regarded as the lost city of the Incas, it's the most visited site in Peru and was named one of the world's new seven wonders. It's an invisible site from the Urubamba valley below, and an agricultural terrace and natural springs surround it.

Inca Trail

Inca Trail is a popular hike in the world. The trail is 42km long and runs through the Andes Mountains to connect Machu Picchu and Aguas Caliente. Tourists go there annually to hike the trail with beautiful scenery, including Inca ruins, cloud forests, and jungles. May-Sept is the best month for hiking.

Did you know

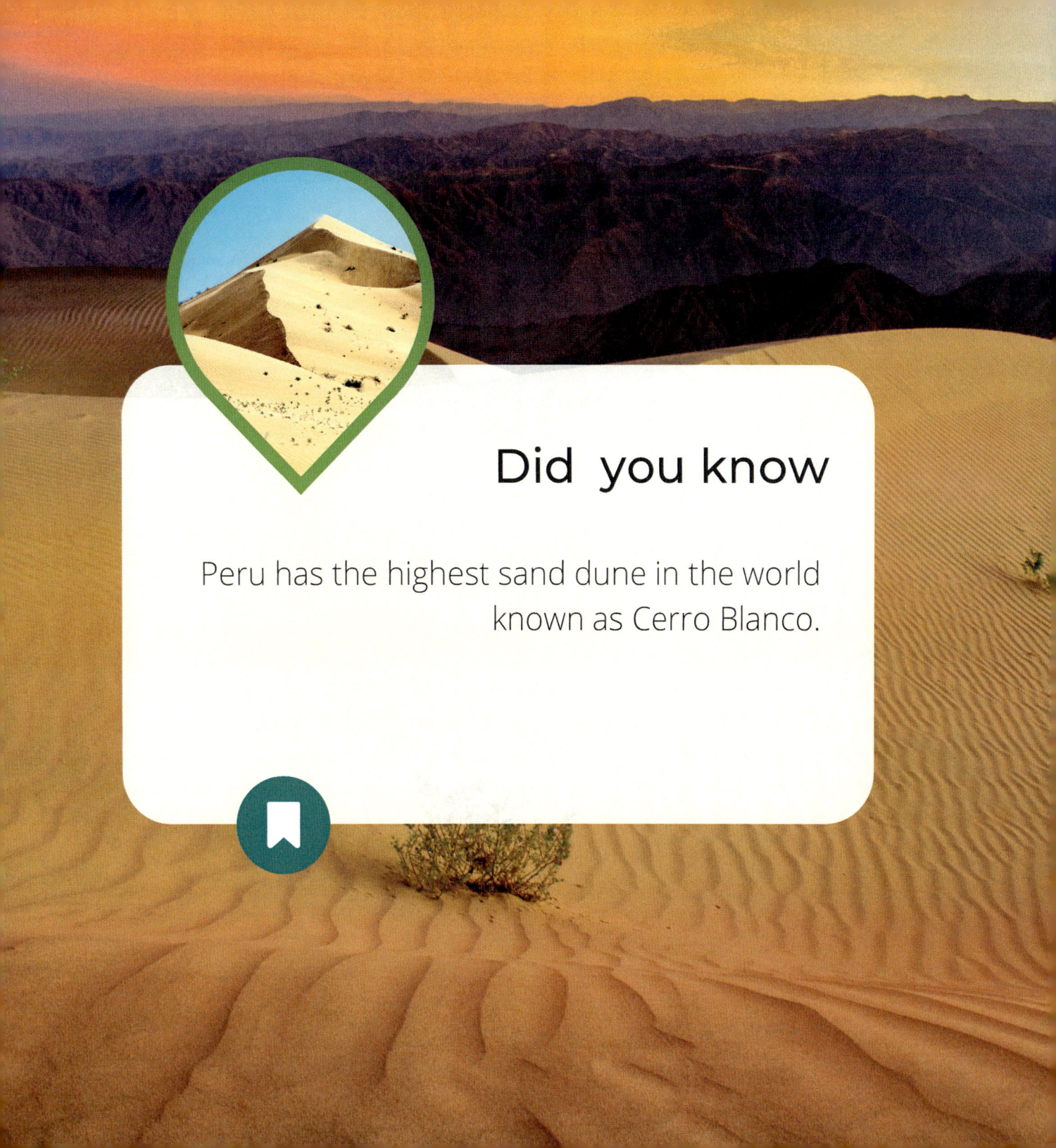

Peru has the highest sand dune in the world known as Cerro Blanco.

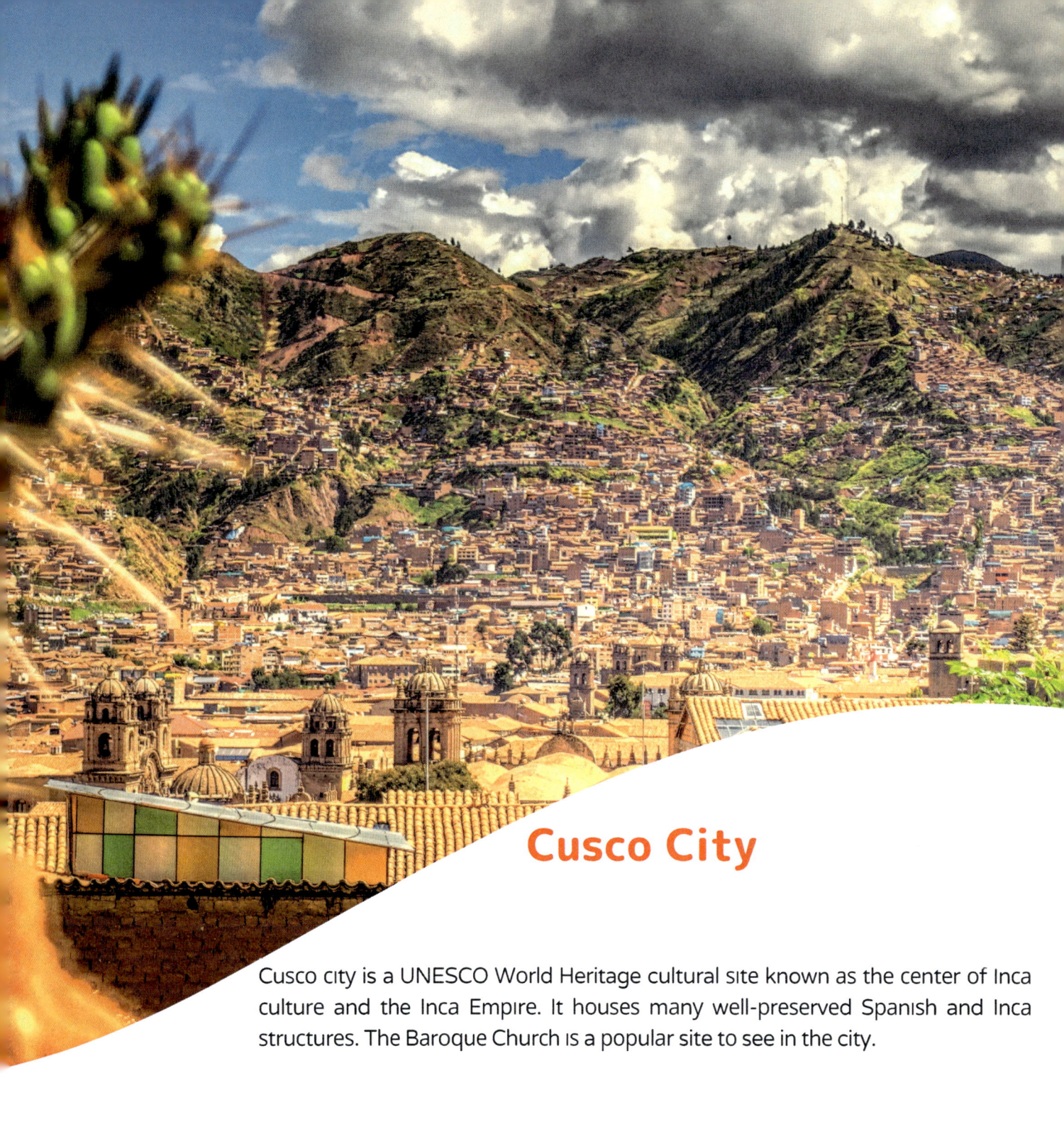

Cusco City

Cusco city is a UNESCO World Heritage cultural site known as the center of Inca culture and the Inca Empire. It houses many well-preserved Spanish and Inca structures. The Baroque Church is a popular site to see in the city.

Huascaran National Park

The Huascaran National Park is part of Cordillera Blanca of Peru, the highest tropical mountain range in the world. Huascaran is a UNESCO World Heritage site and a go-to destination for trekkers and nature lovers.

Historic Center of Lima

Lima is the best-preserved part of the capital city of Peru. The buildings in the historical center of Lima have stood tall for several years after encountering havoc and natural disaster. Lima was the capital for the Spanish when they colonized South America and is home to colonial architecture and elegant structures showing both local and Spanish designs.

Taquile Island

Rather than representing natural and cultural value, Taquile Island is a UNESCO World Heritage site that focuses on textile art. It is cited as an Oral and Intangible World Heritage Site. The textile weaving tradition has existed since the ancient Inca, Pukara, and Colla Civilizations.

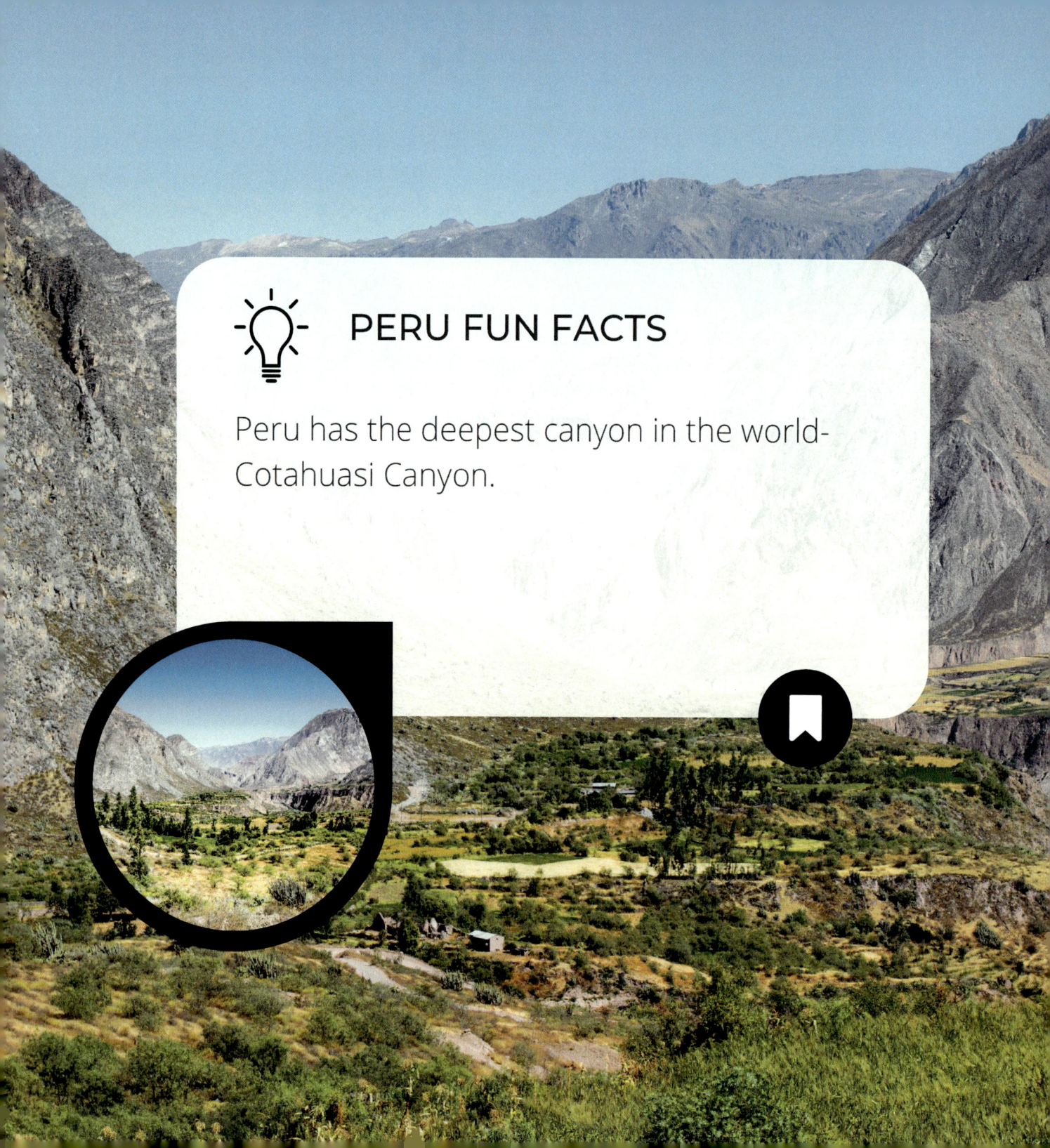

PERU FUN FACTS

Peru has the deepest canyon in the world- Cotahuasi Canyon.

Festivals

Peru has many festivals and events annually. They celebrate every festival with big celebrations and activities.

Popular annual events and festivals

Carnival- A nationwide celebration at the start of Christian lent every February. The festival features planting trees filled with gifts and then dancing around them.

Peruvian Paso Horse Festival- A festival to celebrate the Peruvian Paso horse that was first bred three centuries ago. There are riders on the horse for the national competition.

Inti Raymi- Annual June festival to celebrate the sun, an important entity in Pagan religions.

Corpus Christi- Annual Religious festival in Cusco every 60 days after Easter.

International Spring Festival - A festival celebrating the Peruvian tradition mixed with hundreds of years of Spanish history.

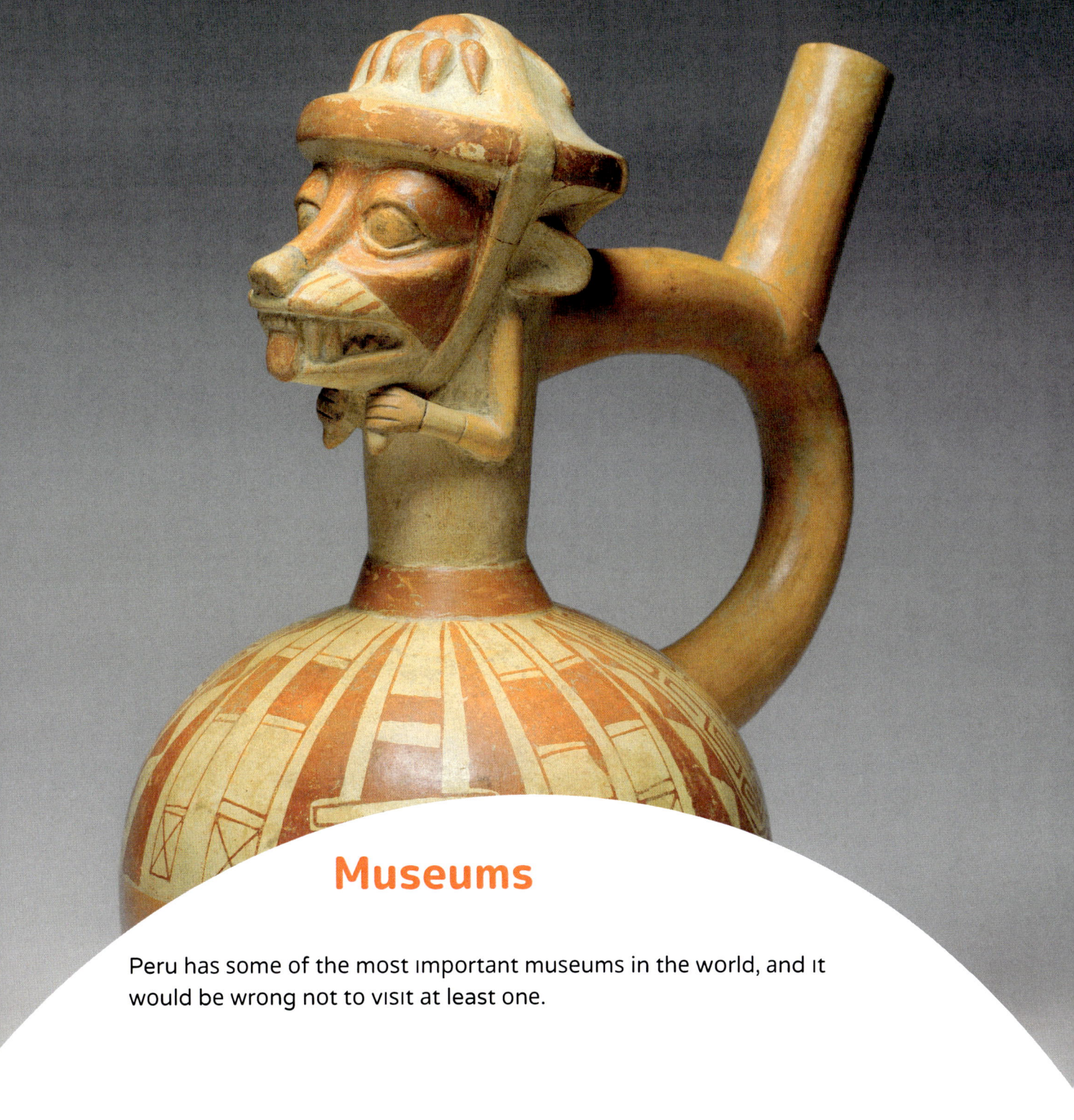

Museums

Peru has some of the most important museums in the world, and it would be wrong not to visit at least one.

Museo Larco

Located in the Pueblo Libre district, the Museo has a wide range of collections of pre-Columbian art that date back thousands of years ago. The museum is notable for its collection of ancient erotic pottery and more than 40000 artifacts.

Museo de Arte de Lima (MALI)

MALI, also known as the anagram of LIMA, houses the largest collection of paintings, pottery, photography, artifacts, and decorations in LIMA. It has 3000 years of Peruvian textiles, photography, and more.

Museo Amano, Lima

The Museo Amano comprises a wide collection of pre-Columbian textile arts and lace. It's an ideal site for history lovers to explore the rich textile past of Peru.

Museo de Osma

Located in the Barranco district of Lima, this museum contains a fine collection of paintings in Peru. It boasts portraits, religious images, and landscapes of the top-rated artists in the country.

PERU FUN FACTS

The tallest flowering plant in the world, Puya Raimondii, also known as the "queen of Andes," is found in Peru.

Food and Dining

Food is never a problem in Peru, no matter where you go. The fertile high-altitude Andes is home to potatoes, corn, and quinoa. There are varieties of potatoes and corn in Peru. The country also grows many fresh fruits and vegetables because of its rich fertile land. The Amazon jungle also covers a large part of the country, so there are many tropical and exotic fruits from the forest.

The population of Japanese and Chinese immigrants has also had a great influence on Peruvian food. You'll find a lot of Chinese restaurants and food in the cities. Pizzas, hamburgers, and sandwiches are available everywhere. Some popular food includes falafel, Neapolitan-style pizza, anticuchos, potatoes, fruit juices, simple roast chicken, and french fries.

Accommodation

Peru has the usual range of Latin American accommodation. There are luxurious international hotels, basic rooms, rustic homestays, camping, and campsites. There has also been a rise in the midrange option, shaping the growth of international and domestic tourism in the country.

Transportation

The options for transportation are numerous. From trains to buses you are faced with quality options to travel around the country. Here are transportation options in Peru..

Bus

For long-distance transportation, buses are the leading option in Peru. Generally, the services are poor but can be better if you travel with top-end companies.

Train

Trains are not common in Peru like road transportation. However, they are much safer, offering a smooth and spacious ride with luxury cabins.

Mini Bus

Mini-buses offer affordable means of moving around big cities in Peru. The only shortcoming is the frequent stops at bus stops which can delay the ride.

Plane

If you want to travel fast and safely in Peru, flights are the best option.

Boats

You might likely take a boat with Peru because of the number of oceans and rivers within the country's surroundings. Boat transportation is adventurous and will let you have a good view of the country.

Colectivos

Colectivos or shared taxis are similar to regular taxis but carry four passengers and have set fees. They are suitable for short trips, and prices are low in cities and towns.

Shopping

Peru is a commerce-booming nation. There are many shops, boutiques, shopping malls, and commercial areas where you can buy things within your budget. Lima, the capital city, is the home to many shopping outlets in the nation. Many international brands and boutiques have their stores there. Larcomar is considered the best place to shop in Lima.

When to Visit Peru?

The best time to visit Peru is the dry season between (May-October). The temperature is pleasant with sunny days and bright blue skies. You'll have time to explore most of the country. It's a peak season so consider booking ahead.

Rainbow Mountain at Vinicunca, Peru